INTRODUCTION

Dangers and abuses are pandemic in every age, but it is healthy to be aware of the particular challenges of our current time. This way we will know what kind of lifeline to look for. And Christianity is unique in offering hope and a positive response to every evil there is, including sin and death.

The cross is our answer to fear. And to every loss. By turning curses into crosses we enter into the Christian victory over sin, death, and all their causes and consequences.

Christians are not different in what we suffer, only in the way we suffer. We have a different focus. Christians see everything as an opportunity to grow in union with God through faith, hope, and love, which we recognize as the goal and fulfillment of life itself. For us, crucifixion is inseparable from resurrection, temporary pain from eternal ecstasy. That is the specific and unique key to the way Christians respond to suffering.

As a practical suggestion, when making the Stations of the Cross, we should "see how the divinity hides itself" (Saint Ignatius). God does not treat his sons and daughters on earth like privileged children. Instead, God keeps us in solidarity with the human race, as Jesus chose to be. That is the key to the incarnation of Jesus and to its continuance in us.

> *Let the same mind be in you that was in Christ Jesus, who, though he was in the form of God, did not regard equality with God as something to be exploited, but emptied himself… taking the form of a slave.… And being found in human form, he humbled himself and became obedient to the point of death—even death on a cross.* • **PHILIPPIANS 2:5–8**

As we contemplate the fourteen moments of Christ's Way of the Cross, we will see how the principles above offer hope and a positive response to the particular challenges of our time.

THE FIRST STATION
Jesus Is Condemned to Death

RESPONSE
to FALSEHOOD

LEADER   The First Station: Jesus is condemned to death. *[pause]*

When he was judged, Jesus confronted the reality of the falsehood and deceit that prevail in our world. He was condemned by people who chose to believe lies over obvious truth.

We adore you, O Christ, and we bless you.

ALL   Because by your holy cross, you have redeemed the world.

LEADER   Isn't this a characteristic of our times? Political commentaries reek of lies, spin, and overt hatred. Advertisements manipulate rather than inform. News channels show slant, not sincerity. People are excluded by gossip, fired, even condemned to death unjustly. This is a blight in our time.

How did Jesus respond to falsehood? Specifically, to the lies that sent him to death?

[pause]

Jesus spoke truth to the Sanhedrin and Pilate. But he didn't argue where it was useless. He accepted falsehood as a fact but with confidence the truth would prevail. He said, "For this I came into the world," not to prevent people from lying, but "to testify to the truth" (John 18:37). That is the Christian response to falsehood.

It is enough. We can live in peace with that.

READER "If they have called the master of the house Beelzebul, how much more will they malign those of his household! So have no fear of them; for nothing is covered up that will not be uncovered, and nothing secret that will not become known. What I say to you in the dark, tell in the light; and what you hear whispered, proclaim from the housetops" (Matthew 10:25–27).

[pause for silent prayer]

ALL Lord, when lies and chosen ignorance distress me, let your response to unjust condemnation remind me to simply bear witness to the truth. Amen.

THE SECOND STATION
Jesus Takes Up His Cross

RESPONSE *to the* CONSEQUENCES *of* SIN *in* OUR TIME

LEADER   The Second Station: Jesus takes up his cross. *[pause]*

Christians believe we have a call from God to "take up our cross" (see Matthew 16:24). This means bearing with redemptive love those consequences of the sins of our time that happen to fall on our shoulders.

We adore you, O Christ, and we bless you.

ALL   Because by your holy cross, you have redeemed the world.

LEADER   Are we not overwhelmed almost daily by the suffering caused in our world by sin? Violence, poverty, private crime, and public corruption—we face these every day. Is our only reaction anger and frustration? Or can we accept what we cannot change, as Jesus accepted the cross?

[pause]

For Christians, everything is beneficial. We just need to turn curses into crosses by adding in meaning through faith, promise through hope, and value through love. We know, as Jesus did, that the cross we are carrying can give life—to us and to the world.

READER Jesus said, "You have pain now; but…your hearts will rejoice….In me you can have peace. In the world you face persecution. But take courage; I have conquered the world!"…. Father…as you sent me into the world, so I have sent them into the world…so that the love with which you have loved me may be in them, and I in them" (John 16:22–33, 17:18, 22).

[pause for silent prayer]

ALL Lord, when I am faced with pain and distress, open my heart to its meaning through faith, its promise through hope, and its value through love. Amen.

THE THIRD STATION
Jesus Falls the First Time

RESPONSE *to* DISILLUSIONMENT

LEADER The Third Station: Jesus falls the first time. *[pause]*

There is nothing lower than corruption in high places.

We adore you, O Christ, and we bless you.

ALL Because by your holy cross, you have redeemed the world.

LEADER Jesus falls. And he was God. How do we feel when those we looked up to and followed as the best and brightest, fall into temptation and sin?

[pause]

Jesus couldn't sin, but he could fail. When he fell under the cross, his human weakness hid his divinity. We have to remember that divine humans can still be weak, and sinful humans can still be divine. No one is purely good or purely bad. So we keep following leaders who limp, as long as they are leading in the right direction.

READER "Simon, listen! Satan has demanded to sift all of you like wheat, but I have prayed for you that your own faith may not fail; and you, when once you have turned back, strengthen your brothers....I tell you, Peter, the cock will not crow this day, until you have denied three times that you know me" (Luke 22:31–32, 34).

[pause for silent prayer]

ALL Lord, let me show equal compassion for saints and sinners. Amen.

THE FOURTH STATION
Jesus Meets His Blessed Mother

RESPONSE *to* SORROWING PARENTS

LEADER   The Fourth Station: Jesus meets his Blessed Mother. *[pause]*

Who can imagine how parents suffer with their children?

We adore you, O Christ, and we bless you.

ALL   Because by your holy cross, you have redeemed the world.

LEADER   When Jesus saw his mother, there was no reproach in her eyes. She understood why he had to suffer. But through her he also saw the eyes of other mothers asking his Father, "Why?" "Why did my child die, end up in jail, become addicted to drugs, leave the Church, suffer a heartbreaking divorce? Why? Where were you, God?"

What would your answer be?

[pause]

To overwhelming grief there is no answer but silence and shared tears. But we need to know God shares them. God takes responsibility for making people free, knowing that inevitably some would misuse freedom to bring suffering on themselves and others. And when they do, we see how God feels about it in the passion of his Son. Looking into his eyes, Mary saw the pain Jesus felt for all parents' pain. And we see the pain God feels for ours.

READER Then Simeon blessed them and said to his mother Mary, "This child is destined for the falling and the rising of many in Israel, and to be a sign that will be opposed, so that the inner thoughts of many will be revealed—and a sword will pierce your own soul too" (Luke 2:34–35).

[pause for silent prayer]

ALL Lord, it is only by your gifts of faith, hope, and love that Mary could accept your pain and hers. I too have these gifts. Help me to use them to find solace for myself and others. Amen.

THE FIFTH STATION
Simon of Cyrene Helps Jesus Carry His Cross

RESPONSE *to* POVERTY *and* NEED

LEADER The Fifth Station: Simon of Cyrene helps Jesus carry his cross. *[pause]*

Faced with anyone bearing any cross, the first impulse of a Christian is to help carry it.

We adore you, O Christ, and we bless you.

ALL Because by your holy cross, you have redeemed the world.

LEADER We know in our hearts that the Romans were moved to get help for Jesus because Mary prayed for it. But was Simon resentful? Did he feel Jesus was faking exhaustion? That he brought his suffering on himself?

What do we feel when forced to pay taxes to help the needy? Do we judge they are taking advantage? That they themselves are responsible for their condition? How unconditionally should we help those in need?

[pause]

We are called to a love that is prudent, not enabling. But Jesus said, "Just as you did it to one of the least of these who are members of my family, you did it to me" (Matthew 25:40). Christians see the poor as family. And more—as the body of Christ. That gives us a different perspective.

READER A man fell into the hands of robbers, who beat him, and went away, leaving him half dead. A Samaritan saw him, and was moved with pity. He bandaged his wounds, and took care of him. Jesus asked, "Who do you think was a neighbor to the man who fell into the hands of the robbers?" "The one who showed him mercy." Jesus answered, "Go and do likewise" (see Luke 10:29–37).

[pause for silent prayer]

ALL Lord, let me love before I judge those who are in need. Amen.

THE SIXTH STATION
Veronica Wipes the Face of Jesus

RESPONSE *to* DEGRADATION

LEADER   The Sixth Station: Veronica wipes the face of Jesus. *[pause]*

In degraded humanity, Christians see Jesus disfigured.

We adore you, O Christ, and we bless you.

ALL   Because by your holy cross, you have redeemed the world.

LEADER   When Veronica saw the swollen face of Jesus oozing sweat and blood, she wanted to restore his true image. This should be our reaction when we see the image of God defaced in human beings, either by others' treatment of them or by their own conduct. What do we feel when we encounter rudeness or vulgarity, racial brutality or dehumanizing incarceration? Do these make us want to help people "clean up their act"? This can be a response of love for Jesus Christ.

[pause]

We have two reasons to feel for others what Veronica felt for Jesus—they are human beings like ourselves, made in the image of God, and they are Christ's body. Our first thought when we encounter anyone should be Paul's watchword. He said it summarized everything he was sent to preach: "Christ in you, the hope of glory."

READER Jesus said, not only, "You shall not murder, commit adultery, or steal," but also, "You shall love your neighbor as yourself" [see Matthew 19:18–19]. To love is to want others to be and to be everything they can be, both as humans and as the body of Christ.

[pause for silent prayer]

ALL Lord, show me your face. Where it is disfigured, help me restore it. Amen.

THE SEVENTH STATION
Jesus Falls the Second Time

RESPONSE *to* DEFECTIONS *from the* CHURCH

LEADER   The Seventh Station: Jesus falls the second time. *[pause]*

It distresses us that so many today answer "none" when asked about their religion.

We adore you, O Christ, and we bless you.

ALL   Because by your holy cross, you have redeemed the world.

LEADER   Anyone can fall into sin. Moses, David, Peter—all did, and badly. But they didn't give up on God or on themselves. And God used them to serve his People.

But Jesus knew that many, discouraged by the repeated failures of so many Christians, or by their own inability to find life in his disappointing Church, would give up on him in his sinful humanity. They would look for him in his divinity alone. But that makes the real Jesus unrecognizable, because the Word made flesh only exists as both human and divine. In his present body on earth, that means both saintly and sinful.

A "pure Church" is pure illusion—but only until the "wedding banquet of the Lamb," when Jesus will present his Church "holy and without blemish, as a bride adorned for her husband." Until then we persevere by "dreaming the impossible dream." And working to make it come true.

[pause]

Jesus fell the "second time" (which can mean all the times between the first and last) to call back those who have given up. No matter how ineffectual his humanity might be, in himself or others, Jesus never gives up on it. Neither should we.

READER   Let us lay aside the sin which so easily ensnares us, and run with endurance the race that is set before us, looking on Jesus, the author and finisher of faith, who endured such hostility against himself from sinners, so that we may not grow weary or lose heart (see Hebrews 12:1–3).

[pause for silent prayer]

ALL   Lord, don't let me ever stop seeing you—in myself and in the community that is your stumbling humanity today. Amen.

THE EIGHTH STATION
Jesus Meets the Women of Jerusalem

RESPONSE *to* WELL-INTENTIONED IGNORANCE

LEADER The Eighth Station: Jesus meets the women of Jerusalem. *[pause]*

The women were sincerely sorry for Jesus—but out of context. He told them they didn't see the big picture.

We adore you, O Christ, and we bless you.

ALL Because by your holy cross, you have redeemed the world.

LEADER People today are focusing on single issues in politics and in the Church, while ignoring what is really destroying both nation and religion. We may feel strongly about the need to make abortion a crime as well as a sin, or to ordain women, or to stop persecuting LGBTs, or to enforce the rules. But, right or wrong, none of these addresses the real corruption in the Church and world, which is the failure to converse with God and each other in the light of faith. To ignore the cause is to invite the effects. Jesus warned the women about this.

[pause]

When Satan can't get us to do evil, he tries to focus us on the lesser good instead of the greater. He focuses us on making laws. Jesus tells the women to focus on the deeper causes that brought about his death.

READER "Daughters of Jerusalem, do not weep for me, but for yourselves and your children. For the days are coming when they will say to the mountains, 'Fall on us!' and to the hills, 'Cover us!' For if they do these things in the green wood, what will be done in the dry?" (see Luke 23:28–31).

[pause for silent prayer]

ALL Lord, open my eyes. Save me from tunnel vision. Amen.

THE NINTH STATION
Jesus Falls the Third Time

RESPONSE *to* HOPELESSNESS

LEADER The Ninth Station: Jesus falls the third time. *[pause]*

How often do we give up because we think things will never change?

We adore you, O Christ, and we bless you.

ALL Because by your holy cross, you have redeemed the world.

LEADER We can accept almost any failure, in ourselves or others, if we believe it is the last one. But how can we know that? Jesus didn't know his third fall was his last one. What made him keep getting up was his commitment to the Father, who was calling him to keep going, no matter how weak he was. And his love for us, which was unconditional.

Jesus accepts us unconditionally. He will never stop trying to unite us to himself in perfect faith, hope, and love. And that is how we must accept the human-divine body of Jesus on earth—pitiful in its sinners, fabulous in its saints, but always able to respond divinely—one more time.

When others' sins, or our own, become so vivid or painful to us that we "just can't take it anymore," we need commitment to the real Jesus, human as well as divine.

[pause]

It is never logical to give up because of what humans do or don't do. Jesus came to call sinners. If we don't accept others who keep sinning, what hope do we have for ourselves?

READER   Since we are justified by faith, we have peace with God through our Lord Jesus Christ, through whom we have... hope of sharing the glory of God....And hope does not disappoint us, because...while we were still weak...Christ died for the ungodly. Rarely will anyone die for a righteous person— though perhaps for a good person someone might....But God proves his love for us in that, while we still were sinners, Christ died for us (see Romans 5:1–8).

[pause for silent prayer]

ALL   Lord, don't let me misjudge you by judging those you came to save. Amen.

THE TENTH STATION
Jesus Is Stripped of His Garments

RESPONSE *to the* PUBLIC EXPOSURE *of* SIN

LEADER The Tenth Station: Jesus is stripped of his garments. *[pause]*

It hurts us to see Jesus stripped naked today, the sins of his body laid bare to the world.

We adore you, O Christ, and we bless you.

ALL Because by your holy cross, you have redeemed the world.

LEADER We are tempted to cover up, to close our eyes to sins in our society and in the Church—especially those that might make any group we identify with look bad to others. We have learned, however, that cover-ups are not only useless but sinful. So how do we deal with exposure?

[pause]

By taking flesh, Jesus stripped off the glory of his divinity and "emptied himself" by becoming like us in every way except sin.

Now, however, although guiltless himself, Jesus is shamed by the sin in his human body. We are his body. Our sins are the sins of his flesh. Jesus accepts and suffers that his body should be stripped bare and seen as it is. Every sin of ours strips Jesus of visible glory.

READER   Christ Jesus, though he was in the form of God, did not regard equality with God as something to be exploited, but emptied himself, taking the form of a slave, being born in human likeness. And being found in human form, he humbled himself and became obedient to the point of death—even death on a cross (Philippians 2:5–8).

[pause for silent prayer]

ALL   Lord, let me bear my humiliation and the humiliation of your people as you did, but with determination to reform myself and help others do the same. Amen.

THE ELEVENTH STATION
Jesus Is Nailed to the Cross

RESPONSE *to* FAITHLESSNESS

LEADER The Eleventh Station: Jesus is nailed to the cross. *[pause]*

Can we have confidence today that people will live up to their commitments?

We adore you, O Christ, and we bless you.

ALL Because by your holy cross, you have redeemed the world.

LEADER In our world, we take for granted that business people cheat, politicians break promises, and some priests and bishops live double lives. Newscasters report selectively with spin. Under pressure, our friends may turn on us. Even divorce, though sometimes justified, is commonplace. We have reason to fear that people will jettison any commitment that becomes a cross.

Jesus let himself be nailed to his cross. What does that express?

[pause]

In the Garden Jesus surrendered his divinity to the Father: "Your will be done!" Now he lets his humanity be rendered powerless. Nailed, he cannot escape the cross without a miracle. His answer to broken promises is to make it humanly impossible for him to break his own.

When Christians are committed to their cross, the nails that hold them are faith, hope, and love. When tempted to give up, we should make ourselves as conscious of each of these as Jesus was of the nails in his hands and feet.

READER Those who passed by derided him, "You who would destroy the temple and rebuild it in three days, save yourself! If you are the Son of God, come down from the cross." In the same way the chief priests, scribes and elders, were mocking him, saying, "He saved others; he cannot save himself. If he is the King of Israel; let him come down from the cross now, and we will believe in him…." The bandits who were crucified with him also taunted him in the same way (see Matthew 27:39–44).

[pause for silent prayer]

ALL Lord, let the faith, the hope, and the love you give me be as strong as the nails that held you on the cross. Amen.

THE TWELFTH STATION
Jesus Dies on the Cross

RESPONSE *to* SUFFERING *in the* WORLD

LEADER The Twelfth Station: Jesus dies on the cross. *[pause]*

It is mind-boggling that Christians, to show Jesus to the world as the Way, the Truth, and the Life, would present him as crucified.

We adore you, O Christ, and we bless you.

ALL Because by your holy cross, you have redeemed the world.

LEADER Suffering is not the way we want to follow, the truth we want to contemplate, or the life we want for ourselves or for anyone we love.

Yet it was what God the Father chose for his beloved Son.

People thought the Messiah was going to take suffering out of the world. Instead, Jesus took the suffering of the world on himself and allowed sin to kill him. And we present him, on the cross, as the Way, the Truth, and the Life! Why?

[pause]

The answer is that what we see on the cross is not just a crucified body, but the expression of faith, hope, and love. That is the "life to the full" that Jesus came to give (John 10:10). Christ's crucifixion is the divine love of God made visible in human flesh.

Anything that lets us live faith, hope, and love is the Way, the Truth, and the Life.

READER Darkness came over the whole land until three in the afternoon. At three o'clock Jesus...gave a loud cry and breathed his last. And the curtain of the temple was torn in two, from top to bottom. Now when the centurion, who stood facing him, saw that in this way he breathed his last, he said, "Truly this man was the Son of God!" (see Mark 15:33–39).

[pause for silent prayer]

ALL Lord, open my eyes to see the mystery of love you revealed on the cross. Amen.

THE THIRTEENTH STATION
Jesus Is Taken Down from the Cross

RESPONSE *to* RETIREMENT

LEADER   The Thirteenth Station: Jesus is taken down from the cross. [*pause*]

Retirement is a challenge for many. Both death and retirement raise the same question. When we come down from the cross of our labor, we ask, "In the last analysis, was my life in this world worth anything?"

We adore you, O Christ, and we bless you.

ALL   Because by your holy cross, you have redeemed the world.

LEADER   When Jesus was taken down from the cross, it seemed clear his life had been a failure. Jesus had changed nothing in Israel. Few believed in him. His disciples had deserted him. Poverty and oppression were rampant, peace non-existent. Two thousand years of Christianity have brought about great progress—but when Jesus died, nothing was accomplished that people expected of the Messiah—nothing that Jesus himself was taught by his culture to expect. All he saw was failure.

[*pause*]

Christians believe in the promise: "I chose you...to go and bear fruit." We know God succeeds in us, in spite of our failures.

READING "I am the true vine, and my Father is the vinegrower....Every branch that bears fruit he prunes to make it bear more fruit....Abide in me as I abide in you.....Those who abide in me and I in them bear much fruit, because apart from me you can do nothing....I have said these things to you so that my joy may be in you, and that your joy may be complete" (John 15:1–11).

[pause for silent prayer]

ALL Lord, you created me to bear fruit in this world. Let me trust, not in what I see, but in "every word that comes from the mouth of God." Amen.

THE FOURTEENTH STATION
Jesus Is Laid in the Tomb

RESPONSE *to* DEATH

LEADER The Fourteenth Station: Jesus is laid in the tomb. *[pause]*

Burials focus us on loss—of the presence of loved ones, or of what they might have experienced had they spent more time on this earth. And every burial reminds us our own existence here is limited—and might end at any moment. What does Christ's burial tell us?

We adore you, O Christ, and we bless you.

ALL Because by your holy cross, you have redeemed the world.

LEADER Christ's burial tells us that, even in Christian burial, the appearances are misleading. We are not burying our loved one, not putting anyone in the ground. We are just burying the physical remains of someone who is not dead, but much more alive than we are—who now has unrestricted enjoyment of the fullness of divine life we all received at baptism.

We know this because, when Jesus was put into the tomb, he came out again to prove it.

[pause]

Every funeral should be for us a joyful celebration of life, as we give thanks that none of the appearances are real. We are conscious, however, that the physical separation from loved ones is real, though temporary, and can be a great suffering, as it was for Mary, the Sorrowful Mother.

READER "I am the bread of life...that comes down from heaven, so that one may eat of it and not die....Whoever eats of this bread will live forever....Those who eat my flesh and drink my blood have eternal life, and I will raise them up on the last day" (see John 6:48–58).

[pause for silent prayer]

ALL Lord, give me faith in the life you give. Amen.

CONCLUSION

LEADER We have walked the Way of the Cross with Jesus. But it doesn't end here. We pray that what Jesus experienced as the Way, the Truth, and the Life, while carrying his cross, we will experience as long as we carry ours.

(Suggestion: If praying these stations as a group, ask a different reader to read each item below).

Lord, when we are appalled by the falsehood and deceit that prevail in our society, let the unjust judgment passed on you move us, like you, simply to testify to the truth.

Lord, when we have to bear the consequences of sin in the world, let us accept our suffering as you did, and turn curses into crosses by adding meaning through faith, promise through hope, and value through love.

Lord, when we are disillusioned by corruption in high places, let your first fall teach us that divine humans can still be weak, and sinful humans can still be divine.

Lord, when we see parents suffering for their children, let us see in your eyes, as you met your sorrowful mother, the pain God feels for all parents' pain.

Lord, when we resent being forced to help the needy, let us find, in Simon shouldering your cross, an awareness of being one family with the poor.

Lord, when we see your image defaced in human beings, move us, by Veronica's example, to reveal your beauty in them.

Lord, when the mediocrity of believers tempts us to stop gathering with the Church, let us learn, through your repeated falls, to accept human weakness without capitulating to it.

Lord, when single-issue politics and narrow religion blind us to the essentials you focused on, let your warning to the women of Jerusalem alert us to the dangers we ignore.

Lord, when sheep and shepherds alike keep falling into sin, and needed reforms seem hopeless, let your refusal to give up, no matter how often you fell, remind us our trust is in God.

Lord, when the sins of your people are laid bare to the world, let your acceptance of nakedness convince us that the only way to life is truth.

Lord, when commitment seems a thing of the past, let us see, in the nails that fixed you to the cross, that faith can keep us faithful, if we have hope and love.

Lord, when fear of suffering threatens our peace, move us to look at you on the cross. Anything that calls us to greater faith, hope, and love is the Way, the Truth, and the Life.

Lord, when awareness of failure diminishes our joy, let us look at your body being lowered from the cross, and realize that your whole life appeared to be a failure when you died. We believe our lives bear fruit, not because we see it, but because you promised they would.

Lord, when death appears to be separation and loss, let the placing of your body in the grave assure us that appearances are deceptive. Death is entrance into the fullness of life, of union, and of joy.

LEADER Finally, Lord, let us see clearly that your Way of the Cross is the true way: the Way of Truth and of Life.

Let us go in peace.

ALSO BY DAVID M. KNIGHT

A Fresh Look at the Our Father
Rediscovering the Power of the Lord's Prayer
96 PAGES | $12.95 | 5½" X 8½" | 9781627856768

Examination of Conscience Guided by the Holy Spirit
32 PAGES | $2.95 (bulk pricing available) | 4" X 6" | 9781627856669

A Fresh Look at Confession
Why It Really Is Good for the Soul
128 PAGES | $12.95 | 5½" X 8½" | 9781585959013

30 Days on the Mass
Reflections and Inspiration on How We Celebrate
32 PAGES | $2.95 (bulk pricing available) | 4" X 6" | 9781627853101

The Mystery of the Cross
Praying the Stations with Pope Francis
32 PAGES | $1.95 (bulk pricing available) | 5½" X 8½" | 9781627852456

Praying the Stations of the Cross for Healing
32 PAGES | $1.95 (bulk pricing available) | 5½" X 8½" | 9781627854931

Ways of the Spirit
Using the Gifts, Showing the Fruits
144 PAGES | $16.95 | 5½" X 8½" | 9781627855976

TO ORDER CALL 1-800-321-0411
OR VISIT WWW.TWENTYTHIRDPUBLICATIONS.COM

TWENTY-THIRD PUBLICATIONS
A division of Bayard, Inc.